MA COMÉDIE

ma comédie

POEMS

C O N N O R B J O T V E D T

OUTPOST PRESS
ABIQUIU, NEW MEXICO

OUTPOST PRESS

Published in 2025 by Outpost Press
Cover Design and Interior Design by Connor Wolfe
Cover Image © Lytovchenko Olexandr, *Kharon*
TRADE PAPERBACK 978-1-965320-41-9

10 9 8 7 6 5 4 3 2 1

Look for our titles in paperback, ebook, and audiobook wherever books are sold.
Wholesale offerings for retailers available through Ingram.

Outpost Press is committed to ecological stewardship.
We greatly value the natural environment and invest in conservation.

TABLE OF CONTENTS

h

o

m

m

e

à

l

a

m

e

r

i.

Mark Antony!
Blest, comely Cleopatra!
      Will your progeny!

Salaryman!
Pitiable Hack! {Samson!}
      Weave your seaman's yarn!

Oh, Elijah!
Oh, great Anachronism!
    Herald the Judgement!

Salaryman!
{Proselytizing dandy!}
    Belay your croaking!

Fair Beatrice!
Fine instrument! {>Possession!<}
    Be Orchestrated!

Salaryman!
Pestiferous scrutineer!
    Shore up your moorings.

ii.

Thunder! Lightning!
Quick! Scramble the beachcombers!
    Please, rescue my craft!

Salaryman!
*Unshackle the Libertines!**
    *—The Old Debauchees!**

Stop! Pilferers!
You: Thieves! Scoundrels! Privateers!
    Please, unhand my men!

Salaryman!
Cowardly homunculus!
    Stand on your tiptoes!

Mary Celeste!
My future; Carried away!
      Please, Jove, release them!

Salaryman!
Chin up: 'Hands at ten-and-two!'
      Raise the dead elsewhere.

iii.

Puissant tease!
Celebrated bon vivant!
      Please, revive my clique!

Salaryman!
Abandon the metaphor!
      Bon—joie de vivre!

Impressionist!
Apologetic Waffle!
        Please, spare me the row!

Salaryman!
Delectable Myrmidon!
        Injudicious Trout!

Vulgarian!
Pigheaded Rhetorician!
    Please, quell the maelstrom!

Salaryman!
Rage against the dominion!
    Lambaste the Author.

iv.

Shepherd! Shepherd!
Summon my compatriots!
    Summon Phlegyas!

    Salaryman!
    Spy: The Plutonian shores!
        Hideous jongleur!

Tremoring Babes!
Unsupplied for all this time!
      Please, sack the storehouse!

Salaryman!
unconscionable Castrate!
      Blasphemous poltroon—

{Silence} Shylock!
Sly, Cantankerous parrot!
      Please, Jove, muster them!

Great Quixote!
{Capitan!} Look, what this way comes!
      Venerites! Gentiles!

v.

{exquisite Wit!
Well, ineloquent Patois:

     Secure my passage!}

Salaryman!
Linger among the Idle,

     the Morbid Stable!

> *Machiavels!* <
Mallards! Egrets! {Prolepses!}
> *Flock!* < {~~*Literatim.*~~}

Salaryman!
{Alas!} Their Standing-Orders!
——*Fastidious Pricks!*

Ferrous pillars!
Stalwarts! {Languorous fibers!}
   Slip into my hand!

Salaryman!
So much for the afterlife!
   Merry, are the men.

vi.

>Time!< Prospero!
Mischief Maker! {Mister Hughes!}
   Please, pardon the State!

         Salaryman!
        Pardon Me, "Mighty Sumer!*
          Bestir the Waters!"

*Controversy!**
{Sage!} fabled Inquisitor!
Please, sharpen my Tool!

Salaryman!
*{Lonesome Mariner!} Sexton!**
Desert the Undead!

Father!
—Infinite-stellar-plexus!
Please, unbridle Me!

Salaryman.
Tightly-packaged-tinderbox!
Extinguish yourself.

vii.

nourishing eau,
once invigorating spring;
  please, bear! {Temperance!}

    Salaryman.
    Rise! Rise to the occasion!
     Rise! Tempered Phoenix!

*commanding mein,
once infatigable stone;
      please, bear! {Fortitude!}

Salaryman.
Rise! Rise, powerful Stanchion!
      Rise! Fortified Sup!

*languishing palm,
once indispensable seed;
please, Janus! {Prudence!}

Salaryman.
Rise! Rise, undulating Spume!
Rise, gentle Poet.

viii.

Felon! >Felon!<
To arms: Schooners; balladeers!
       Avast, ne'er-do-wells!

       Salaryman!
       Surely, He accommodates!
         Send for Charles-H'nri!

*Son-of-a-Bitch!**
Rapturous heart, cease Bleating!
       Please, grant Me courage!

         Salaryman!
       "Kingdom, Glory, and the horse!"—
           profuse, profound Shroud!

Winsome Reaper;

inscrutable Egotist;

      Please, excuse the dogs;

      Salaryman!

      "Paymaster!" *{~~"dutiful Hand!"~~}*

        Execute the Lot!

b

o

u

é

e

ix.

Salaryman!
{that damnable quagmire;}
       Where are your bootstraps?

in-peace, Witness!
   Witness, Glory! *{Witness, Grim.}*
      My hands! *{Consolate.}*

Salaryman;

cheery-spectre; Resurrect;

       manifest your Will!

                                       {Pacifier!}

                                   >Feaster of this wretched lot!<

                                         {Wolf-in-sheep's-clothing!}

Salaryman;
earnest-shade; Regenerate;
        stow your Bellyache!

        ~~esteemed-Virgin,~~
        politicking-bitch!* {Strumpet;(!)}
            Fetch me my Compass!

x.

Salaryman;
endure, endure your hardship(s)!
           Providence atones.

first-Register!
{untwist-my-reddening-flesh!}
           "{oh!} unlatch your Purse!"

Salaryman:
{a-principled-pick-pocket?}
 —a-wily-Tomcat!

first-Conduit!
{breathe-anywhere-but-my-neck!}
 "{oh!} Condescension!"*

Salaryman:
{a-forsaken-Nightingale?}
    —a-sankebit-Heelhound!

first-Aquifer!
{wipe-the-sweat-from-off-my-brow!}
    "{oh!} reveal my Path!"

xi.

Salaryman,
>Avert your troublesome gaze!<
> *>Roll away the stone!<*

great-Architect!
great-Remnant-of-Babylon:*
> *{Aye!} babbling-Nimrod!*

Salaryman!
{Aye!}~Pompous~Forget~me~Not! *
        >poor-Empedocles!<

great-Diviner!
great-Appollonian-fig; *
        make clear your meaning!

~~Salaryman;~~
churlish-Scoundrel;* {Reprobate;(!)}
>Shoo away your ghosts!<

~~{great-Prospector!}~~
~~{great-Envy-of-King-Midas;(!)}~~
a pearl, and nugget…

xii.

{Aye!} *Turgid saints;**
Marshalls. > {*Hemmed-to-the-Mainsail;(!)*} <
    "*Men, Speak a good word!*"

~~{Aye!}~~ *Barrackers!*

Lampoons!* > {Fashioned-to-the-Jib;(!)} <

"~~Men!~~ Speak a good word!"

{aye.} flaky-Tarts,
deplumed by-the-hand-that-feeds. . .
"Men. ~~Speak a good word.~~"

xiii.

difficult-Pill;
~~*{And taken-with-the-bitters!*}*~~
    Yes, Hamlet, "to be."

natural-Hoop;

~~*{And ridden-with-great-contempt!*}*~~

Yes, Richard, "a horse."

unblemished-Pines;

~~*{And trod-with-your-clumsy-mind!*}*~~

Yes, William, "the stage."

xiv.

Salaryman!
{that infernal harborage;}
        Where is your Bondsman?!

                                    *concealing-Port;**
                                    the-Burgundy-Valley!
                                            {Aye;} Shipmaster, ho!

Salaryman!
You imprudent-émigré:(!)
　　　Where are your Scruples?!

blund'rnig-Nomad;
{Opposite-the-Crimson-Field!}*
　　Shipmaster, your mark!

Salaryman!(!)
{You would approach the blockade?}
　　　Where is your Good-form?!

　　　　　　　　　　　　　immortal-husk,
　　　　　　　　　　　　　suffer-the-indignancy:(!)
　　　　　　　　　　　　　　　"arise, Lazarus."*

la

historia de los caballeros

i.

Soñador…
{Acostado en la luz…}
　　¡Feo, el Hierro!**

　　　　　　　　　{¡Ay!}——¡Chico!**
　　　　　　　¡Espera! > {¡Esperame!} <
　　　　　　　　　¿Has visto la Dam——?

"¿Dam–? la Dam——?"
~~*>{¿Dame paciencia?}<*~~**
>*{¡Dame tu Nombre!}<*

{Maestra,}
{¡Vírgen de Guadalupe!}
~~*{¿Está perdida?}*~~
>*la Dam——¡Madonna!<***

¡Soñador!

¿Qué dijiste—"¡Madonna!?"

> *¡Ay!—¡Estás loco!***

¡Palurdo!

¿Dónde está el Autor?—

> *¡¡Sí, él.¡ >El Bufón!<***

ii.

{¡ey!}—¡Inglés!
¿Adónde vas, la Torre?**
        {¡Dílo—'Princesa!}'

{¡Ay!}—¡Feo!
{¡No arrastres los Pies!}**
        ¡Lanza tus Flechas!

{¡ay!}—*¡Inglés!*
¡No me malentiendas!
   {¡dime Su nombre!}**

          {¿ey?}—*¿Feo?,*
       y ¿de qué te serviría?—
           >{¡Un Chauvinista!}<**

*¡Soy Feo!***
Valiente y Noble…

    ¡Un Escudero-!

      ~~*¡¡-de Escudero!}*~~

       ~~*pues, perdón;*~~

      *{¡Y qué Sombra Proyectas!}***

        ¡el Topo del Rey!

iii.

{¡ay!} —¡Inglés!
{¿Y tú, el Juez Supremo?}**
>*¡huelo Mierda!<*

¡Cuidado!
{¡Arruinarás tu cena!}
¡Tapa tu Nariz!**

{¡ay!} — *¡Inglés!*
¿Por qué atormentarme?**

        >~~*¡déjame hablar!*~~<

{¡ay!} — *¡Feo!*
Porque estoy gravado —

        >~~*{¡con esa boca!}*~~<

        ¡Descansa tu Voz!**

Inglés…

"p—*Cuéntame sobre Ella:*

~~{algo Concreto…}~~"**

~~{¿Concreto?}~~

"h—*Niño, Cierra tus ojos:—*

¿*No puedes Verla?*"**

iv.

Ingles,
{¡mis Pies doloridos!}**
        Debo descansar…

¡Feo!——
>{¡Que Griten para Sangre!}<**
        ¡Continuarás!

Ingles,
¿Cuándo puedo Vislumbrar?—
          {¿La—la Sirena?}**

          ~~¡Feo!~~
¿Qué dijiste—"¡Sirena!?"
          >~~{¿S—Una Medusa?}~~<**

¡Ingles!
¡Basta de Metáforas!**
>~~*¡¡Los Misterios!}*~~<
¡Ya Aprendido!

Feo;
Si quieres la Verdad,——**
Reza a Jonás.

v.

Ingles:

¿A quién, El Pescador?**

¡Ay!—¡Está muerto!

¡Feo!

{¡Sí, Veo tu dilema!}**

¡te Falta la fe!

¡Ingles!
¿Qué fe?——¿Fe en los Muertos?——
        ¿los Ciego,**Cojo?

¡Dios!*
{¡Créanos un Poeta!} ——
        >{¡un Peregrino!}<
        {¡Haznos un Bastón!}**

~~Ingles...~~

¿De qué estás hablando?—

       ¿San Patricio?**

~~Feo;~~

¿y Prevés Serpientes?—

       ¿en los Árboles?**

vi.

{~~¿Árboles?~~}

{~~¿Estas,~~ estas *Malezas?*}

>{¿~~¿e══Tallos de Maíz?!~~}<**

{*ay, Feo;*

**{*Humilde y Podrido*—

{*un escudero… […]*

¡Ingles!

>*¡Has Perdido el Camino!*<**

>*{¡y Tu Cabeza!}*<

Feo:

¡No he Perdido Nada!

*Lo recordaré…***

¡Ingles!

¡Mira Allí y Allá!—

~~{¡Allá y Allá!}~~**

> {¡no Veo nada!} <

Feo:

~~pues,~~ Cómprame un Asno,**

y despídete.

vii.

~~*¿un Asno?*~~
{¿la Bestia de Carga?} —

    {¡Ja!} — *¿Y tus Cargas?***

    ¡Feo!
{Cargada o Sin Carga} —

      ¡no Se quejará!**

~~¡Ingles!~~
¡Por favor, mi Pellejo!
      {¡Dejarás marcas!}**

~~{Feo}~~
{¿Con tu Cuello grueso?}
      ¡y Tu Cabeza!**
      {Aún más gruesa …}

¡Ingles!

{¡Ay!}——¡No me Reprendas!**

    No entiendes…

Feo:——

~~*{a las Manos de Dios}*~~

    ¡Comprometerse!**

viii.

"*¡Madonna!*—
~~*{¡me He Librado de él!}*~~ **
¡Déjame verte!"

"¡Madonna!——

~~{¡He llegado tan Lejos!}~~

¡Déjame verte!"**

"¡Madonna!——
~~{¡no Dejaré de Buscar!}~~ **
~~{¡Aquí o Allá!}~~
déjame verte…"

la

confesión

ix.

{{Albañil}}—
{{Has llegado tan Lejos}}
  {{Déjame Verte}}**

"¡Madonna!—
{{¡Ay!}}==>¡mi Cuerpo tiembla!<
  {¡Que hermosa Voz!}"**

{{Albañil}}—

{{H̶a̶s̶ ̶l̶l̶e̶g̶a̶d̶o̶ ̶t̶a̶n̶ ̶L̶e̶j̶o̶s̶}}

      {{no Puedo verte}}**

"¡Madonna!—

>{¡Estoy Delante de Tí!}<

      ¡̶A̶y̶!̶═¡A tus pies!

      >{¡En Mí Espada!}<"**

{{no me importa}}

{{¡a la Mano del Pastor!}}

> *{{y Su Cuchillo}}* < **

*"¿y Así?——***

> *{¿me Abandonarías?}* <

> *¡me Prometiste!* < *"*

x.

{{Vago}}**

{{limpia tus lagrimas}}

    {{no te escondas}}

"Pastor…

>{¡Jurado y Verdugo!}<**

    Gloria a ti…"

{{Vago}}
{{ahórrame tu fila}}
  {{salva tu Lengua}} **

"*Pastor…*
>{¿un Absolucionista?}< **
Te pido perdón…"

{{Vago}}.
{{te rozas con la muerte}}
       {{brazo y muslo}}**
       {{eres un tonto}}

"Pastor...
>{¡un ~~Médico Sabio!~~}<**
       ¿Qué debo hacer...?"

xi.

{{Vago}}
{{la luz esta menguando}}
        {{Tu veredicto}}**

"¡Pastor!
>{¡Tomador de Boletos!}<
        ¡Otro Momento!"**

{{Vago}}
{{El Anfitrión espera}}
        *{{Su tripa gime}}***

"*¡Pastor!*
>*{¡Maldito Mayordomo!}*<
        >*¡Los incendios!*<
        {y los Rojizos…}'''**

{{Vago}}
{{todos están sentados}}
      {{esperando Ti}}**

{{Pastor,}}
">¡Portero Ansioso!<
      ¡No Estoy Listo!"**

xii.

~~{{la luna}}~~
{{la mañana se vuelve}}
{{Vago—no hay fin.}}**

~~{Pastor}~~
>¡Redactor de Palabras!<
...Darles la vuelta..."**

{{~~Vago~~}}
{{ay, no te Avergüences}}
   {{pon tu Mejilla}}**

       {~~Pastor~~}
      ">¡estrella Oriental!<
        >¡soy Bendecido!<"**

{{Albañil}}**

{{no causar disturbios}}

    {{cierra tus ojos}}

    {{junta tus manos}}

    'Sra. Parca,

    {Para tí;} Sí, Para tí.**

      Me comprometo…"

xiii.

{{Albañil}}
~~*{{camina junto a mi}}*~~
     {{habla conmigo}}**

"Sra. Parca,
¿Qué significó todo?——
        ¿~~la suma~~, el Fin?"**

{{Albañil}}
~~*{{se formarán grietas}}*~~
  {{cuida tus pies}} **

'*Sra. Parca,*
{¡Esta tierra delgada!},
  ~~*>{¡Me Ahogaré!}<*~~ **
  >¡Dame tu Mano!<

92

{{Albañil}}

{{Marinero** por favor…}}

{{suelta la cuerda}}

"Sra. Parca,

Canción del Piélago;**

Canta para Mí."

xiv.

{{Náufrago}}**
{{cuerda deshilachada}}
      ~~*{{hilo marchito}}*~~

{{Náufrago}}
{{casco desmoronado}}**
~~{{casquijo flojo}}~~

{{Náufrago}}
~~*{{mercader maltratado}}*~~
    {{el empleado}}**
    {{pudrirse al sol}}

l

a

m

b

i.

preliminary.
secondary, satellite
repository.

ii.

and on the first day,
and on the seventh, the fifth—
    time is perplexing.

iii.

on; and off; and on:
and so was the age of man!
terrestrial woe.

iv.

and then came Caesar!
woe; upon woe; upon woe:
    plagues and pestilence.

v.

Yea, unleash the wise!
crooked scoundrels, and the like!
siege after sieges.

vi.

westward expansion:
oh! how it tortures the mind!
my empty stomach…

vii.

fish are vanishing.
the ice mourns its extinction.
my mind turns, and turns…

viii.

the wheels of progress!
the carrousel of mankind!
decaying orbits.

ix.

cyclicality.
gravitational forces.
    their paltry offspring.

x.

I need a mother.
the touch of something sincere:
anyone will do.

xi.

> *a hand helping hands!*
> *I should have been a father:*
>   *anyone would do.*

xii.

at its terminus,
a moment is at best obscure…
      ~~discretionary.~~

xiii.

laughter lights the world
and I could extinguish it.
everybody dies.

xiv.

extermination:
the end of all living things.
　　I am so sorry.

ABOUT THE AUTHOR

Connor Bjotvedt, a Tucson-based public school teacher, is an accomplished poet and scholar. He earned his MFA in Writing from Spalding University in 2018 and a BA in English, Literature, and Creative Writing from Northern Arizona University in 2016. During his time at Northern Arizona, he participated in the local reading series *The Narrow Chimney* and won the Charles E. Bull Creative Writing Scholarship for Poetry. At Spalding, he published his academic thesis *The Politics of Storytelling: Narrative Bias in Maurice Manning's The Common Man* and his creative thesis *A Contemporary Portrait of the Southwest.*

For over a decade, Connor has refined his approach to haiku, transforming the traditional form into experimental micro-poetry and dramatic verse. His creative influences include poets Richard Brautigan and Malena Mörling and songwriters such as Scott Hutchison and Sean Bonnette. Connor's writing reflects a commitment to exploring themes of deurbanization, decolonization, faith, and love, while celebrating the richness of the American Southwest. Through his innovative approach to poetry and storytelling, Connor strives to create art that challenges conventions and uplifts marginalized perspectives, leaving a lasting impression on readers and the literary world alike.

At Wayfarer Books we believe poetry is the language of the earth. We believe words—shaped like rivers through wild places—can change the shape of the world. We publish poets and writers and renegades who stand outside of mainstream culture—poets, essayists, and storytellers whose work might withstand the scrutiny of crows and coyotes, those who are cryptic and floral, the crepuscular, and the queer-at-heart. We are more than just a publisher but a community of writers. Our mission is to produce books that can serve as a compass and map to all wayfarers through wild terrain.

wayfarerbooks.org

OUTPOST
≡PRESS≡

AN IMPRINT OF WAYFARER BOOKS

At Wayfarer Books we believe poetry is the language of the earth. We believe words—shaped like rivers through wild places—can change the shape of the world. We publish poets and writers and renegades who stand outside of mainstream culture—poets, essayists, and storytellers whose work might withstand the scrutiny of crows and coyotes, those who are cryptic and floral, the crepuscular, and the queer-at-heart. We are more than just a publisher but a community of writers. Our mission is to produce books that can serve as a compass and map to all wayfarers through wild terrain.

WAYFARERBOOKS.ORG

www.ingramcontent.com/pod-product-compliance
Lightning Source LLC
Chambersburg PA
CBHW020410130626
46549CB00006B/2504